CACHE Entry Level Certificate

Preparation for Childcare

Ann Tapp

www.heinemann.co.uk

Free online support
Useful weblinks
24 hour online ordering

01865 888118

Heinemann

Heinemann is an imprint of Pearson Education Limited, a company incorporated in England and Wales, having its registered office at Edinburgh Gate, Harlow, Essex, CM20 2JE. Registered company number: 872828

www.heinemann.co.uk

Heinemann is a registered trademark of Pearson Education Limited

Text © Pearson Education Limited 2008

First published 2008

12 11 10 09 08
10 9 8 7 6 5 4 3 2 1

British Library Cataloguing in Publication Data is available from the British Library on request.

ISBN 978-0-435987-40-4

Typeset by 𝌆 Tek Art
Illustrated by 𝌆 Tek Art
Cover design by Siu Hang Wong
Cover photo/illustration © Corbis
Printed in the UK by Scotprint

The author and publisher would like to thank the following organisations for their kind permission to reproduce material: Procter & Gamble (for the use of Always Ultra, p.11); BSI Group (for the use of the Kitemark™, p.73); The British Toy & Hobby Association (for the use of the Lion Mark, p.73)

Every effort has been made to contact copyright holders of material reproduced in this book. Any omissions will be rectified in subsequent printings if notice is given to the publishers.

Acknowledgements
To start with, a huge thank you to Beth Howard, for her support and guidance during the writing of the book and the publishing team for a superb job in producing the text. Thank you also goes to my family: Rod, Christian and Adrian, for their technical support and help with the initial word-processing.

Ann Tapp

Contents

Unit 3
Playing and learning in the home

Introduction

This textbook has been designed for the CACHE Entry Level Certificate in Preparation for Childcare course. It will be helpful for anyone who is starting to study childcare at a basic level.

Features of the book

- The book has three units that match the units of the CACHE course.
- At the start of each unit is a glossary of the important words you will meet in that unit.
- Each unit is split into topics on double-page spreads.
- There is a list of Key Points and an Activity idea included on most double-page topic spreads.
- For each Activity you will find a reference to the Key Skills area that is covered, e.g. **Com** = Communication, **AoN** = Application of Number, **ICT** = Information and Communication Technology.

Author's note

Welcome to your childcare course.

Childcare is a difficult subject to learn because of its many topic areas and all the rules and regulations that need to be covered. Seeing how children develop and learn can be a very rewarding role, whether as a parent or a childcare worker. This textbook will start you on the learning process to become a good childcare worker and will help you if you eventually have your own children.
I hope you enjoy your course.

Ann Tapp

Unit 1 Pregnancy, contraception and the first 12 weeks of a baby's life

Introduction

This unit is all about pregnancy, contraception and the first 12 weeks of a baby's life. You will learn about:

- changes to boys and girls in puberty
- the menstrual cycle (periods)
- how pregnancy happens
- how to tell if you are pregnant
- what medical help you need when you are pregnant
- how a foetus (baby) develops in the womb
- the birth of a baby
- staying healthy when pregnant
- eating healthily when pregnant – foods to avoid
- dangers of smoking, alcohol and drugs
- the father's role
- birth and immediate care
- aftercare of mother and baby
- contraception and sexual health
- the responsible parent – where to get help
- being a good neighbour.

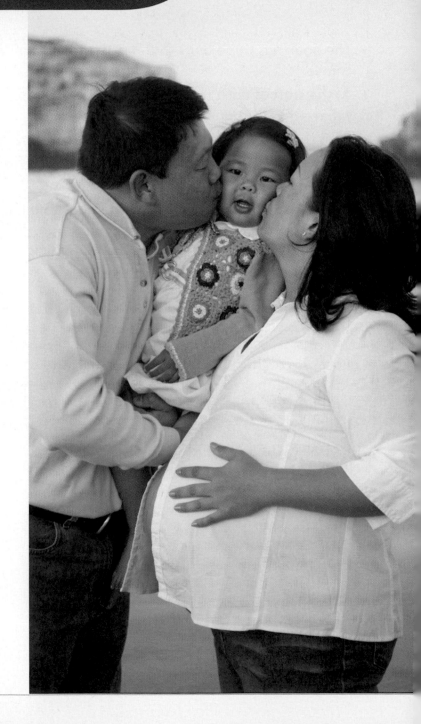

Glossary

Here are some of the words you will meet in this unit. Some of them may be new to you.

- **Contraceptive** – something you use to stop becoming pregnant
- **Embryo** – the new life that develops after the egg and sperm meet
- **Fertile** – describes a woman who is at the right stage of her menstrual (period) cycle to be capable of becoming pregnant
- **Fertilisation** – when the sperm meets the egg and joins with it
- **Foetus** – a baby is called a foetus while in its mother's uterus (womb)
- **Hormones** – chemicals made by the body that control certain things that happen in the body, such as puberty
- **Menstruation** – this is when the blood lining of the uterus (womb) is shed, usually about once a month – we call this 'having a period'
- **Nutrients** – things we need to eat to stay healthy, including proteins, carbohydrates, vitamins, minerals and some fats
- **Ovulation** – when an egg is released by the ovary – this usually happens halfway through the menstrual cycle
- **Placenta** – a large organ that develops in the uterus (womb) during pregnancy and links the blood supply from the mother to the baby. (After the baby is born, this is called the afterbirth.)
- **Puberty** – when a young person's body starts to become adult. During this time a person undergoes physical, emotional and sexual changes and becomes able to have children
- **Uterus** – the place in a woman's body where a baby grows, also called the womb
- **Womb** – another name for the uterus

Puberty

How do our bodies change at puberty?

At the age of about 12–13 years for girls and 14 years for boys, we reach a time called puberty. This marks the beginning of sexual maturity. The body undergoes many changes that enable sexual reproduction to occur. These changes enable a man and a woman to have children.

The changes that happen in your body start with chemicals called hormones. At puberty your body makes more hormones. Then it starts to produce the sex cells called ova (eggs) in girls and sperm in boys.

Changes to the body

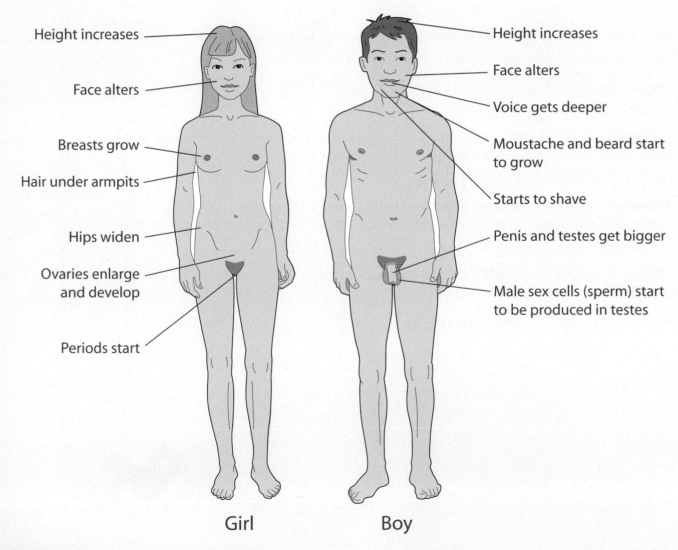

Height increases

Face alters

Breasts grow

Hair under armpits

Hips widen

Ovaries enlarge and develop

Periods start

Height increases

Face alters

Voice gets deeper

Moustache and beard start to grow

Starts to shave

Penis and testes get bigger

Male sex cells (sperm) start to be produced in testes

Girl

Boy

How girls' and boys' bodies change at puberty

Female sex organs

Ovary – a woman has two ovaries, which are attached to the sides of the uterus (womb).

Uterus (womb) – this is the shape of an upside-down pear. It has thick muscular walls and lots of blood vessels in the lining.

Vagina – a muscular tube about 9–10cm long. The concertina folds will stretch when it is time for a baby to be born.

The female sex organs are protected by the bones of the pelvis.

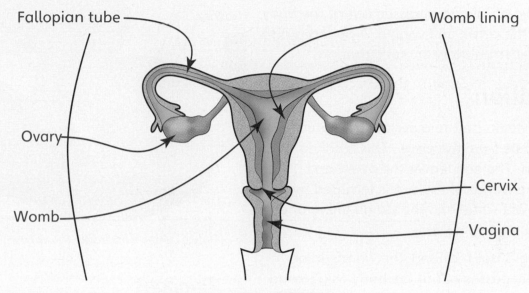

A woman's sex organs

Male sex organs

Testes – equivalent to the ovaries in a female. They produce sperm and the male sex hormone (testosterone). They are found outside the body in a loose pouch.

Penis – usually quite small and soft until sexual excitement. It has a great amount of blood flow, which allows it to become hard – this is called an erection.

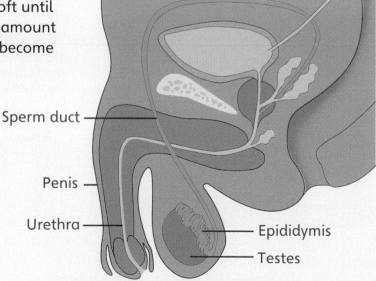

A man's sex organs

The menstrual cycle (periods)

After puberty, women have a period of bleeding about once a month, called a period. Starting to have periods is the single most important change in puberty for girls.

A period happens when a small amount of uterus (womb) lining is passed out of the body through the cervix and vagina. A period is also called menstrual flow or menstruation.

Ovulation

About 2 weeks before a period, the ovum (egg) bursts from the ovary. This is called ovulation. The egg leaves the ovary and enters the womb. If the egg is fertilised by a sperm it will settle into the womb lining and a baby will start to develop.

If the egg is not fertilised, the womb lining eventually passes out of the body as a period.

Sanitary wear

There is a choice of different sanitary protection (things to use when a girl has a period) available.

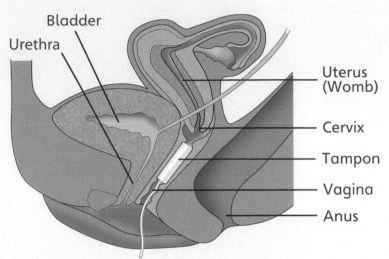

Bladder
Urethra
Uterus (Womb)
Cervix
Tampon
Vagina
Anus

How a tampon fits inside the vagina

Tampons

Tampons are known as internal sanitary protection. A tampon is put into the vagina to soak up the blood from the uterus (womb). Some have an applicator; others are just pushed into the vagina with a clean finger.

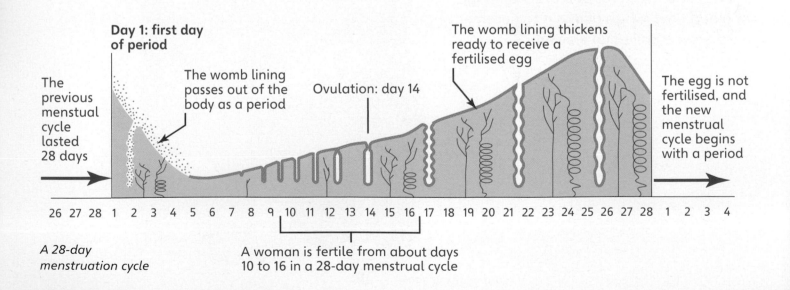

Day 1: first day of period

The previous menstual cycle lasted 28 days

The womb lining passes out of the body as a period

Ovulation: day 14

The womb lining thickens ready to receive a fertilised egg

The egg is not fertilised, and the new menstrual cycle begins with a period

26 27 28 1 2 3 4 5 6 7 8 9 10 11 12 13 14 15 16 17 18 19 20 21 22 23 24 25 26 27 28 1 2 3 4

A 28-day menstruation cycle

A woman is fertile from about days 10 to 16 in a 28-day menstrual cycle

Sanitary towels (pads)

Sanitary towels can be bought with different absorbencies (amount of blood held). Some women have light bleeding and others need a sanitary towel with higher absorbency.

Personal hygiene

It is important to make sure that you keep clean when you are menstruating (when you have a period). Frequent showers are important as you can soon smell unclean. You also need to change tampons and pads frequently.

Make sure you dispose of used tampons and pads correctly – there is usually a disposal unit in a toilet cubicle. Don't put them down the toilet. Always remember to wash your hands.

It is important that you carry some sanitary protection with you at all times if you are not sure of your monthly cycle. This is to prevent you from bleeding on your clothes if you start a period while you are out.

Key points

Personal hygiene is important during a period.

Girls should always make sure they have enough sanitary protection with them, just in case they start a period early.

Activity

1 Design a leaflet for a teenage girl, telling her about the sanitary protection she can choose from when her periods start.

2 Add an explanation of the importance of keeping clean during a period.

Com ICT

You can buy different sanitary towels to suit heavy or light periods

How a woman becomes pregnant

The fertile time of the month

A woman's fertile time is about five days before and two days after ovulation. If she has sexual intercourse without contraception during this time she could become pregnant.

Knowing when your fertile time is

One way you can begin to understand the menstrual cycle better is to use a chart like the one below.

22	23	24	25	26	27	28
1	2	3	4	5	6	7
8	9	10	11	12	13	14
15	16	17	18	19	20	21
22	23	24	25	26	27	28
1	2	3	4	5	6	7

- The chart above is for a 28-day cycle.
- Day 1 is the day your period starts.
- You then count all the days until your next period (the next 'day 1') to work out the length of your menstrual cycle.
- By counting back 14 days from your second period, you can work out approximately when you were fertile.

So, for a 28-day menstrual cycle, ovulation occurs around day 14 and a woman is fertile from day 10 to day 16.

> BEWARE: it is impossible to be 100% accurate as to when ovulation takes place, even if you have a regular menstrual cycle (period). This is why if you don't want to become pregnant, you must **always** use contraception.

Sexual intercourse

For a woman to become pregnant, sexual intercourse (also known as having sex or making love) must take place between a man and a woman, while the woman is fertile.

During sexual intercourse a man puts his penis into the woman's vagina. The movements made by the man and the woman during sex can often result in an orgasm, which is a very pleasurable feeling.

Before sexual intercourse a man and a woman usually touch, stroke and kiss each other (this is called foreplay).

As a man reaches orgasm, about a teaspoon of semen is released (ejaculated) from his penis into the woman's vagina. This contains millions of tiny sperm.

After ejaculation, many millions of sperm die before they reach the egg. Only about 2000 sperm reach the egg, and only one sperm can fertilise the egg.

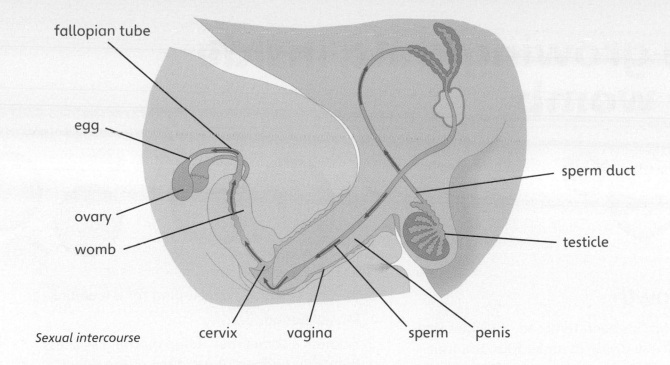

fallopian tube

egg

ovary

womb

sperm duct

testicle

Sexual intercourse

cervix   vagina   sperm   penis

Fertilisation happens when the sperm burrows into the egg.
At this point the sperm and egg join together to make the
beginning of a new life – a baby.

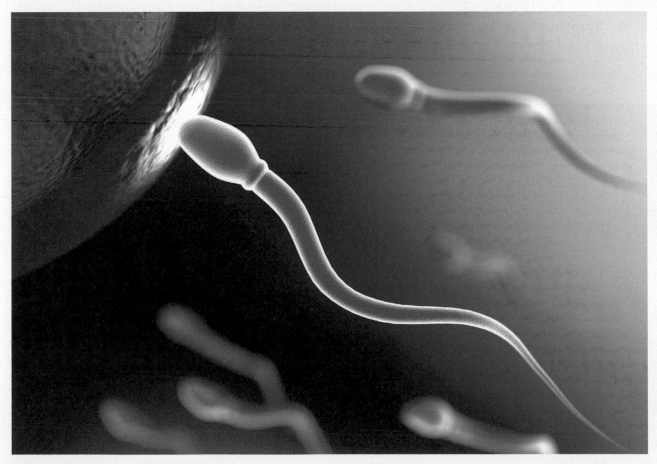

Egg meets sperm – a baby starts here!

The growing child inside the womb

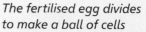

The fertilised egg divides to make a ball of cells

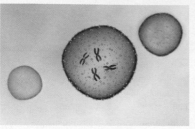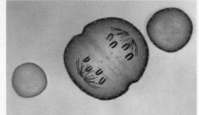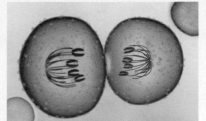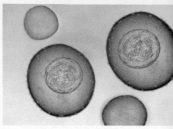

Cell growth

After the egg has been fertilised, it divides into two cells. These divide to make four, the four divide to make eight, and so on until a ball of cells is formed.

When the ball of cells reaches the uterus (womb), it beds itself into the wall of the uterus. This usually happens by day 10 after fertilisation. Once this has happened the woman is pregnant. At this point the cells are called an embryo.

Signs of a new baby developing for a woman:

1. Missed period.
2. Sickness – sometimes called morning sickness but it can happen at any time of the day.
3. Frequent need to go to the toilet to wee.
4. Breasts become heavier, and sometimes ache.
5. Wanting strange foods, such as pickled onions or lemon curd. Some women lose their appetite.
6. Feeling more tired and easily upset.

Pregnancy needs to be confirmed – this can be done using a pregnancy test bought from a chemist, or by a GP or family-planning centre.

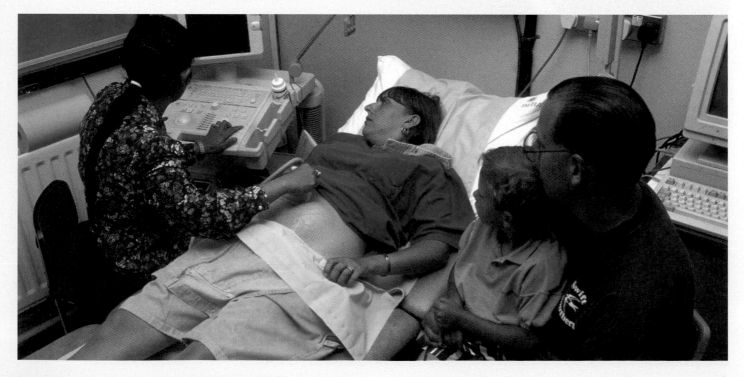

A pregnant woman should have regular check-ups

How a baby develops

Week 6: the embryo grows fast in week six, especially the brain and spinal cord

A foetus (baby) grows very quickly inside its mother. By 6 weeks there is the beginning of a backbone (spine) and the brain is forming. The baby's heart begins to beat. By 12 weeks the foetus (baby) is now easily recognised as a human being.

A human body must have food and oxygen to stay alive, grow and develop. A foetus (baby) will get food and oxygen from its mother through the placenta. The placenta is a special organ that joins the mother and baby.

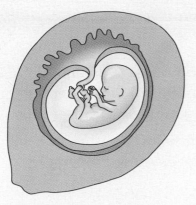

Week 12: the foetus looks like a baby

When the embryo first sticks to the womb lining, it sinks in and starts to be fed through its mother's blood. Soon blood vessels grow and mix with blood vessels from the mother to form the placenta. The foetus is attached to the placenta by an umbilical cord (which makes the baby's tummy button after birth).

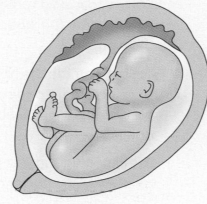

Weeks 18–21: the baby continues to grow, bones begin to develop

In the womb the baby is in a bag called the amniotic sac. This is filled with a watery liquid, which protects the unborn baby inside its mother.

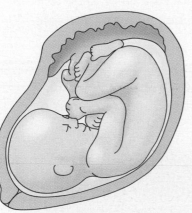

Weeks 27–30: the baby now nearly fills the womb

umbilical cord

placenta

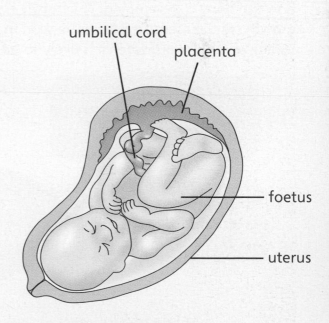

foetus

uterus

Weeks 36–40: the baby has very little space to move around. The baby begins to settle in the pelvis ready to be born

How a foetus develops

The umbilical cord takes food and oxygen to the unborn baby

Staying healthy

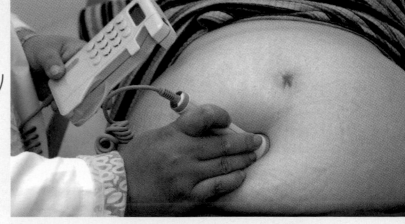

Making sure the mother stays healthy

Pregnancy is a natural process for a woman's body. Most pregnant women can carry on doing what they have always done, but it is important that a pregnant woman takes good care of herself. The healthier she is, the better it is for her, and for the baby growing inside her.

It is important that she visits her doctor regularly. The doctor will check on the development of the pregnancy and be able to advise her on the rest of the pregnancy ahead.

Medical check-ups at an antenatal clinic are also important. Here, a pregnant woman will have her blood taken, be weighed and have a urine sample tested. All these tests help the doctor or midwife check that the baby is growing properly.

Sometimes the doctor sends the pregnant woman for an ultrasound scan. By looking at the pictures from the scan, the doctor can see how the baby is developing. The baby's size and growth can be measured from the scan to assess its age and work out when it is likely to be born.

An ultrasound scan shows how the baby is growing

As well as eating a healthy diet, a pregnant woman may need to take extra supplements to help her unborn baby grow.

Taking folic acid tablets helps to ensure that the baby's spine (backbone) develops properly in the womb.

Taking iron tablets helps to prevent the mother from becoming anaemic – anaemia makes a pregnant woman feel very tired, with no energy at all.

It is important that the pregnant woman listens carefully to the doctor and the midwife. She should ask questions if she is not sure what to do to keep herself and her unborn baby healthy and safe.

Healthy diet

For an unborn baby to grow and develop, it is important that a pregnant woman has a healthy diet.

Don't eat too much sugary or fatty food

Avoid lots of strong coffee, tea or cola as they have high caffeine levels

Drink plenty of water and fruit juice

A healthy diet while pregnant

Reduce the amount of animal fat eaten

Eat lots of fresh fruit and vegetables

Drink milk and keep up a good calcium intake

- Remember that everything a pregnant mother eats and drinks will pass through the placenta to the baby she is carrying.

- Most women gain between 9kg and 12kg when pregnant. It is harder to lose extra weight after a baby is born. Being pregnant doesn't mean you have to eat for two!

A pregnant woman needs to eat healthily, but not too much

A nutritious diet

It is important for a pregnant woman to have a good and varied diet. She should have foods from the five main food groups.

Meat and fish

Fruit and vegetables

Milk and milk products – yogurt, cheese

Fats and oils – butter, margarine and vegetable oils

Cereals and starchy vegetables – bread, potatoes, butternut squash

Key points

There's no need to eat for two – being pregnant doesn't mean a woman has to eat twice as much.

Foods to avoid while pregnant:

Processed food – ready-made meals contain high levels of fat, sugar and salt. Eating food with a lot of sugar in it leads to a high weight gain.

Fried food – this contains high levels of fat. The goodness of the food is lost in the cooking.

Preserved food – for example, smoked fish, as this contains chemicals, additives and a lot of salt.

Remember:

- food should be cooked properly
- food should be not be used after the use-by date
- food should be stored correctly.

Activity

Plan a healthy day's menu for a pregnant woman. You should include breakfast, lunch, an evening meal and snacks.

Com ICT

The dangers of smoking, alcohol and drugs

Drugs

Just as food and oxygen pass from the mother to the baby via the placenta, so do other things.
Some drugs or medications may harm the baby, so it is important that a pregnant woman takes only what her GP says it is safe to take.

Illegal drugs cause harm to both mother and child, especially in the first 3 months of pregnancy. Babies born to drug addicts are sometimes addicted to drugs at birth.

Smoking

It is a well-known fact that babies whose mothers smoke tend to be smaller. Some also have feeding problems, or are more at risk of infections at an early age. Also, it's not good for a pregnant woman to be around other people who are smoking, as passive smoking may cause similar problems.

Smoking affects an unborn baby by reducing the amount of oxygen carried in the bloodstream. If a parent smokes there is a risk of miscarriage, stillbirth (when the baby is born dead) or SIDS (sudden infant death syndrome).

Drugs are dangerous for an unborn baby

Mothers who smoke or drink can damage their babies' health

Alcohol

Pregnant women are advised not to drink alcohol because it travels across the placenta to the unborn child.

Some reasons to avoid alcohol (except for the occasional drink):

- alcohol makes it harder for a woman to become pregnant
- alcohol can increase the risk of a miscarriage in the first 3 months of pregnancy
- if a pregnant woman drinks too much alcohol it can affect the growth and development of her unborn baby
- if a pregnant woman gets drunk she could fall and harm her unborn baby.

Infection

There are a few infectious diseases that can affect an unborn child. One you may hear about is German measles (rubella). If a pregnant woman catches German measles, then her baby may be born blind or deaf, or with other health problems.

Key points

Good nutrients pass through the placenta to the baby. However, bad things like alcohol and drugs – not given by the doctor – also pass through the placenta.

Activity

Design a poster outlining the effects of drugs, alcohol or smoking on an unborn child.

Com

The father's role

As you know, it takes two to make a baby. As the woman gets used to the changes in her body during the 9 months of pregnancy, the baby's father also has to get ready for the new baby.

He needs to be able to understand the physical changes and more importantly the emotional changes to the mother of his child.

The expectant father needs to:

- understand that a pregnant woman can be much more emotional during her pregnancy – she may be upset and cry easily
- provide much more help with housework and gardening, such as carrying heavy shopping bags
- help more with any other children and cook meals when the woman gets tired
- provide support during visits to the GP or the antenatal clinic – most fathers are keen to see their unborn child during scans
- help to decorate the new baby's bedroom and choose clothes and furniture, also help to choose the baby's name
- provide emotional and practical support during the birth of the new baby, hold the hand of the new mother, help with breathing, and encourage pushing.

Once the baby is born, the father needs to become involved in helping to look after it. A good job is taking the baby out for a walk in the pram to give the mother some time to herself.

Fathers can play a big part in childcare

New parents should discuss the ways in which the father can help – it will upset a woman if her partner seems to be taking over and ordering her about.

Both a new mother and a new father will have to adjust to a new baby's routine.

The changes may include:

- sleepless nights
- crying baby
- late meals
- no ironing
- little cleaning.

Key points

Looking after a new baby takes up a lot of time – sometimes new fathers feel left out when a new baby arrives.

Activity

Give examples of jobs a new father could do to help his partner – tips for new fathers.

Com

Babies often need attention at night – being a parent can be tiring

Birth of the baby

Once conception (when a sperm and egg meet) has taken place, a baby grows rapidly. Pregnancy lasts for about 40 weeks.

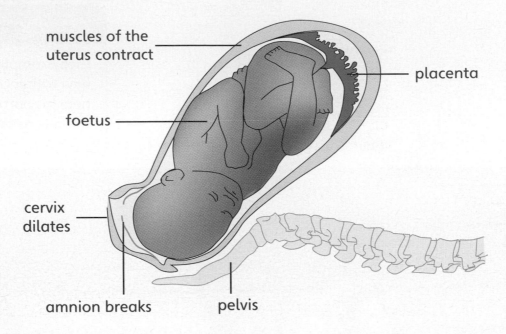

muscles of the uterus contract

placenta

foetus

cervix dilates

amnion breaks

pelvis

At about 36 weeks, the baby gets into position, ready to be born

Some time from week 36 the baby gets ready to be born by moving its head down into the mother's pelvis.

When a baby is ready to be born it is described as being 'full term'; 40 weeks is only a guideline. It is perfectly normal for babies to arrive a couple of weeks before or after the 40-week date.

'Labour' means the process during which the baby is born. The time one woman spends in labour can be very different from another woman. Some babies are born after only a short labour, while others are born after a very long labour.

There are three stages of labour.

The first stage of labour

The opening of the uterus (womb), known as the cervix, widens to give the baby room to come out. The pregnant woman has contractions. These feel like strong period pains; they are a sign that the cervix is opening to let the baby be born. When contractions start, the pregnant woman needs to get to the maternity home for the delivery of her baby.

The second stage of labour

This stage starts when the cervix is fully open (fully dilated) at about 9.5cm. The baby passes out through the vagina (remember the folds of the vagina we talked about on page 9).

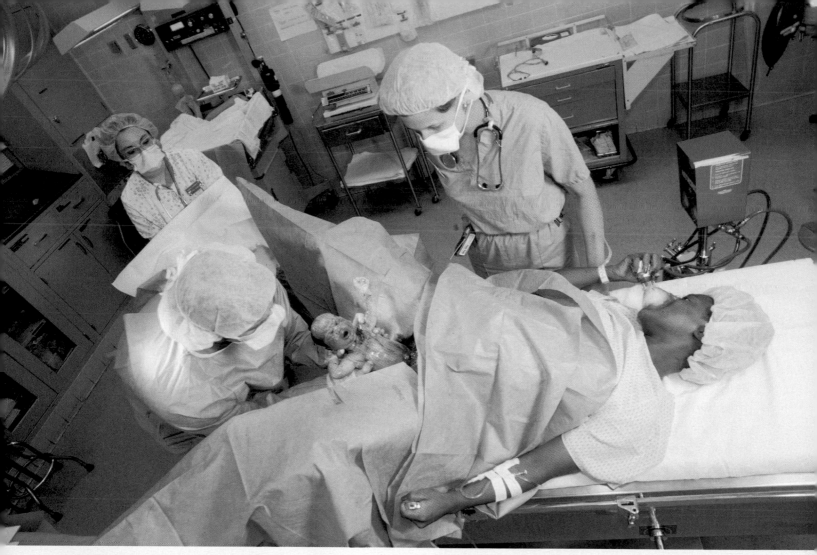

The baby is nearly born

The uterus continues to contract, pushing the baby out. The woman follows instructions from the midwife or the doctor, who are there to help the baby be born and to look after the mother while she is in labour.

The new father is welcome in the delivery room (the room where you go for your baby to be born). He can help and support his partner in labour and see their new baby be born. It can be a very happy time for parents.

The third stage of labour

This stage involves the delivery of the placenta, as the baby no longer needs it.

The midwife and doctor will look at the baby to check that everything is OK. Sometimes babies who are very small will be taken to the special care unit to be looked after carefully.

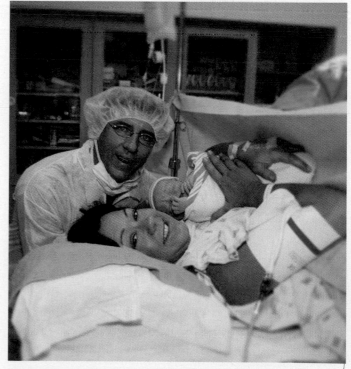

A newborn baby feels safest close to its mother

After the birth of the baby

Once the baby is born, lots of things change. The new baby is completely dependent on its parents for everything. A new mother or father will not be able to carry on living as they did before the baby was born – they will need to think nearly all the time of the new life they are now caring for.

Some of the changes could be:

- Sleep – new babies don't sleep all night, they often wake up and cry and need their mother or father to get up and sort them out, whether it's for a feed, because they are uncomfortable, or because they have a wet nappy.

- Money – babies cost lots of money in nappies, food, clothes and so on – the new parents will have to make sure there is enough money to pay bills as well as provide for the baby.

- Social life – you cannot just decide to go out for a meal or a drink with your friends like you used to – now a baby has to be cared for, so there is the added job of finding a reliable and trustworthy babysitter, and finding extra money to pay them.

- Daily routines – everything has to change to manage the baby. Even a simple shopping trip becomes a huge task – you need to take so much with you to meet the baby's needs, before you even start to shop.

- Exercise – you are tired as the baby is awake for most of the night, and you are behind with the housework – exercise is the last thing you want to do.

A newborn baby is very vulnerable, so it is important to look after it really well in the right way, so that it can grow up healthy and strong.

Mother's milk is the best food for a baby

Feeding the baby

Before their baby is born, most women will decide whether to breastfeed or bottle-feed it.

Breastfeeding is encouraged because of the advantages to the mother and baby:

- there are important nutrients in the mother's milk that help to strengthen the baby's immune system (the immune system helps keep the baby healthy)

- there is no cost for breastfeeding – you don't have to buy bottles or milk powder, or sterilising equipment to keep bottles clean

- it's much quicker to get ready.

Fathers can also be involved in bottle-feeding

Key points

Lots of things change when a new baby is born. Time is no longer your own, as everything you do has to be planned around the new baby.

Activity

1 Design a poster showing the changes new parents need to make for a new baby.

2 Make a shopping list with prices for the things a new baby who is going to be bottle-fed will need.

Com AoN

Sometimes it is not possible to breastfeed, in which case the baby is bottle-fed with milk formula. When bottle-feeding, it is important to keep everything really clean. This helps to stop the baby getting a tummy ache and diarrhoea ('the runs').

Holding the baby

It is really important that when you are carrying a new baby, you take great care that its head is well supported. This is because a baby's head is large in relation to the rest of its body, and its neck muscles are very weak.

Playing with the baby

Babies love it when their carers play with them and talk to them. They like to be able to kick their legs and wave their arms about. Babies from about 12 weeks old enjoy playing with brightly coloured rattles.

Contraception

Contraception is very important

Having a baby can be a wonderful experience, but it can also cause a lot of worry, so you need to make sure you are ready to have a baby. If you decide to have sexual intercourse with a partner, it is important that you use a reliable form of contraception to stop an unwanted pregnancy.

It is the responsibility of both people to choose the best contraceptive method to use to protect each other during sex.

Remember, there are two reasons for using contraception:

- to prevent an unwanted pregnancy
- to protect against sexually transmitted (passed on) diseases.

Attitudes (how people feel) to contraception

Different people have different ideas about contraception. The ideas of the society and culture in which we live can influence what we say and do.

For young people the decision to have sexual intercourse is very important. No one should be forced to have sex or use peer pressure (for example, 'All my friends have had sex') as an excuse to make someone else have sex when they don't want to.

It's important to make up your own mind

If you decide to have sex, it's important to use a contraceptive

Contraception is the responsibility of both people who are having sex. You can get information from a doctor or a family-planning clinic. (Doctors cannot tell anyone why you have been to see them, because you have a right to privacy.) In a chemist the pharmacist can also give advice.

The next two pages show the different contraceptives that you can choose from. Remember that only condoms protect you from sexually transmitted diseases.

The statements below are examples of things people might say about contraception and sex. What do you think about these ideas? Do you agree?

- *He won't go out with you if you don't sleep with him.*
- *It's OK for a man to have sex with lots of women, but if a woman sleeps with lots of different men no-one will want to marry her.*
- *It's too far for me to go to the family-planning clinic and it's too expensive to buy condoms in the shop.*
- *It's against my religion to use contraception.*
- *If I go to my doctor about going on the pill he may tell my mum.*
- *You don't get pregnant standing up or if it is your first time.*

Remember, you **can** get pregnant the first time you have sex. And whether you stand up or lie down – if you don't use contraception you can still become pregnant.

Your doctor cannot tell anyone why you have been to see them, because you have a right to privacy

Different types of contraception

Type of contraception	Who uses it?	How does it work?	Advantages/ disadvantages	What does it look like?
Contraceptive pill	Women	Contains hormones used that stop pregnancy.	Used correctly, the pill is very reliable. However, you must take it regularly – if you forget to take it just once, you could become pregnant. There can also be unpleasant side-effects, such as putting on weight or feeling depressed.	
Contraceptive injection	Women	An injection that releases a hormone slowly into the body to stop ovulation.	One injection lasts between 8 and 12 weeks and is a very effective contraceptive. However, as with the pill there can be unpleasant side-effects.	
Condom	Mostly men and sometimes women	A plastic sheath is placed over the man's penis or lines the inside of the woman's vagina. Condoms are a barrier contraceptive – they prevent sperm from entering the womb.	Condoms protect against sexually transmitted diseases. However, they can sometimes come off or split during sex.	
Diaphragm or cap	Women	Another barrier contraceptive. These are plastic cups that are placed inside the vagina to prevent the sperm from entering the womb.	These must be fitted correctly. They are usually used with a spermicide (a gel that kills sperm) for added protection. They are a less reliable contraceptive. They can sometimes feel uncomfortable during sex.	

Intrauterine device (IUD)	Women	A small T-shaped device made of plastic and copper. It is placed in the womb by a doctor or nurse. It stops sperm from meeting the egg, and also stops a fertilised egg from settling in the womb lining.	Once fitted, an IUD works for between 3 and 10 years. This type of contraception is very reliable, but it is usually only recommended for women who have had children. It can cause women to have heavier and more painful periods.
Emergency contraception ('Morning-after pill')	Women	Several pills are taken over a period of 24 hours, and must be taken within 72 hours of having unprotected sex. They contain a strong dose of hormones to trigger the start of a period. They are available from doctors, family-planning clinics and some hospital departments.	This should be used for emergencies only (for example if a condom splits during sex) and not as a regular contraceptive. It can have strong side-effects.
Sterilisation	Men and women	An operation to make a person unable to have babies. In women, the tubes that carry eggs are blocked. In men, the tubes carrying sperm from the testes are blocked, so that no sperm are produced at orgasm.	Sterilisation is a very effective method of contraception, but it is only for people who are certain they do not want to have more children. After you have been sterilised, it is very difficult and expensive to reverse the operation.

The responsible parent

Once you have a family it is important that you become a responsible parent.

The responsibilities you have towards your child

A parent's responsibilities towards their child

- To provide warmth and shelter
- To provide suitable clothing for the weather
- To provide love and support
- To provide health care when your child is ill
- To protect the child from harm
- To encourage sleep and rest
- To encourage time for play
- To support your child's education
- To read to the child
- To feed and nourish
- To make sure everything the child does is safe
- To help the child understand what behaviour is required
- To help moral development (politeness, saying 'please' and 'thank you')

All parents want the best for their children. Sometimes parents have many questions about how to look after their child in the best way possible. New parents especially may have many questions.

Help is sometimes available from grandparents, family friends or neighbours who have already had children.

Sometimes getting advice from friends or relatives can cause rows if you don't agree with what they tell you, as we all have our own thoughts on how babies and children should be brought up.

Services in the community that can help answer your questions about being a new parent are:

Doctor

Provides medical care for the baby and advice for parents. If the doctor has any concerns about the health of the baby, he/she will send the parents to other health professionals and clinics.

Midwife

Responsible for looking after the health and growth of the baby from birth. Midwives deliver babies, and will also give advice on feeding, sleeping and other things.

Health visitor

Usually works from the baby clinic or the doctor's practice. He/she works with mothers, fathers and children under 5 to help promote health and prevent illness.

Citizens Advice Bureau

A charity that provides free advice on people's rights and responsibilities, and can also offer help with issues of money and housing.

Social Services

Help parents who are struggling to provide suitable care for their children. They also provide protection for children who are suffering from abuse and neglect. They run a fostering and adoption service and are responsible for placing children in foster care or homes.

Gingerbread for single-parent families

A charity that was set up by a single parent to provide help and support for other single-parent families. There is a national helpline and local support groups. You can find its website at www.gingerbread.com.

Key points

A lot of support is available for new parents and single-parent families.

Activity

Design a poster showing what help is available for parents in your area. Try to include a phone number.

Com

Health visitors can give advice on lots of childcare issues

Being a good neighbour

If we all lived on our own with no one else nearby we could live exactly as we liked, but since we live as part of a society we have to consider the people around us, even if we do not know them personally. This is called being a responsible citizen.

For people to work and live close together in society, we need to have rules. From an early age we have rules to follow that are set down by our parents. The rules or laws in society are set down by the people we vote for in Parliament, and who run the Government. These laws are there to help make the place where we live a better place.

Making your local community a better place is good for everyone

People can do all sorts of things to make their local community (where they live) a better place to live. For example, helping people who are less able to support themselves, or helping to keep the community clean.

By working together and helping to look after each other, a good support network is made. This shows that people are trying to be responsible citizens in their own community.

Being a good neighbour means:

- shopping for elderly neighbours or helping your grandparents
- helping by babysitting for friends or relatives
- volunteering for a local charity
- sweeping up leaves or clearing snow for an elderly neighbour
- being thoughtful (considerate) about others when playing your music at night
- making sure your rubbish is put into a bin and not dropped in the street
- being polite.

It is important that you try to be a good neighbour. A lot is written in the newspapers about how young people today cause trouble. Very little is written about young people who help others in society. Wouldn't it be a nice change to see more good news?

Summary of Unit 1

- Personal hygiene is even more important when a woman is menstruating.
- It is important that a pregnant woman follows her doctor's advice.
- A pregnant woman needs to eat healthily.
- A pregnant woman needs to take care of herself and her unborn baby by not smoking, drinking alcohol or taking illegal drugs.
- Being pregnant doesn't mean you need to eat for two.
- Remember that good nutrients as well as harmful things can pass through the placenta to the unborn child.
- New fathers should be encouraged to spend time with a new baby.
- Remember that lots of things change when there is a new baby in the family.
- It is the job of both partners to discuss contraception.
- Condoms are the only contraceptives that can protect you against sexually transmitted diseases.
- Help is available for new parents from many different places.
- Being a good person in society is very important.

Unit 2 Caring for young children from 0 to 3 years 11 months

Introduction

**This unit is all about caring for young children.
You will learn about:**

- personal hygiene
- care of the sick or injured child
- signs of ill health
- accidents in the home and garden
- health and safety inside and outside
- daily routines
- children's hygiene
- a healthy diet for children

- clothes for children (seasonal)
- clothes for baby – layette
- rest and sleep
- the child's bedroom
- bedtime routines
- bathing babies and young children
- bedtime activities
- reasons why bedtimes can be stressful.

Glossary

Here are some of the words you will meet in this unit. Some of them may be new to you:

- **Bacteria** – germs that can make a child poorly

- **Balanced diet** – a good balance of different types of food that will help us to stay healthy

- **Dehydration** – when we don't have enough to drink (e.g. water, milk or juice), the body dehydrates

- **Environment** – the area we are in, for example the classroom environment

- **Germs** – bacteria and viruses. Germs are all around us and unless we are careful they can make us unwell

- **Hazard** – a possible danger, an 'accident waiting to happen', such as a toy on the stairs, that someone might trip over

- **Immune system** – the body's way of protecting itself against illness

- **Non-flammable** – doesn't catch fire. Night clothes should be made from non-flammable material

- **Personal hygiene** – keeping yourself clean, for example washing your hands after going to the toilet, showering or bathing daily

- **Routine** – doing things the same way every time. For example a child's bedtime routine is always the same: bath, teeth cleaning, toilet, story and bed

- **Scald** – burn with liquid or steam, for example with hot water from the kettle

- **Signs and symptoms** – what you can see or feel when you are not feeling well. For example, when a child feels hot and is being sick, these signs and symptoms tell you the child is not well

- **Sunstroke** – illness caused by spending too long in the sun. Children are vulnerable to sunstroke

Personal hygiene

What does personal hygiene mean? Why is it important?

A good standard of personal hygiene helps us protect ourselves and other people. Personal hygiene is important when we are looking after a baby, a young child or anyone else. Children and babies can easily pick up infections because their immune system (what your body uses to resist infection) has not yet developed enough to protect them. An adult's immune system is much stronger.

Personal hygiene means:

- washing your hands after you have been to the toilet
- washing your hands before you prepare food and drinks
- washing your hands after touching animals
- washing your hands after being outside
- always being clean, and having neat fingernails

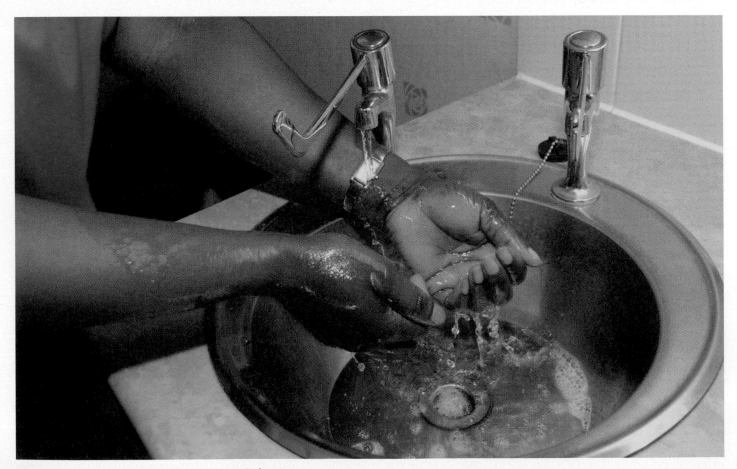

Keeping your hands clean helps to stop infections

- having a shower or bath daily to stop your body from smelling sweaty
- men need to shave or keep their beards tidy
- keeping clothes clean and washing your hair so it is not greasy, also often checking to see if there are any head lice or eggs that need treatment
- cleaning your teeth at least twice a day to help prevent bad breath.

It is really important if you want to work with children, for example in babysitting, that you maintain good personal hygiene. Look at the picture of Glenda and Gregg below – they are going to see if they can get a babysitting job.

Would you give Glenda or Gregg a job looking after children?

Care of the sick or injured child

Just as we all feel ill at times, so do children. Children cannot always explain where they feel poorly or explain what the feeling/pain is like, so it is important that parents and carers learn to look for signs and symptoms of illness in children.

Accidents

Parents and carers need to understand when to get medical help for children.

The following cases need emergency medical help. If the child:

- has swallowed medicine or pills that they shouldn't have
- has breathing problems
- has a broken bone
- has a cut or injury that won't stop bleeding
- has been stung in the mouth
- has a fit or becomes unconscious.

> Remember, you must never give babies or children any tablets or medicine that have not been prescribed (given to them) by a doctor.

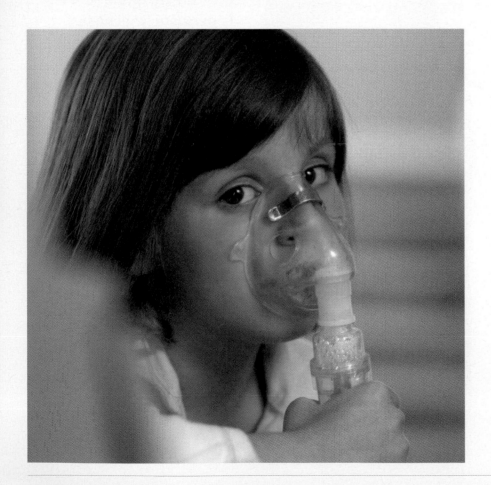

The emergency services are there for when you need help quickly

Some people think it is good fun to ring the emergency services, for example an ambulance, with a hoax (not real) call. This could mean that someone who really needs the ambulance will die, because the ambulance is busy following the hoax call. How would you feel if this was a relative or friend of yours?

It is really important that parents and carers know what to do when a child has an accident, as they might be the only adult around at the time, and may need to get emergency help.

Here are some examples of the types of accidents a child might have while they are in your care, and below are the ways in which you should deal with them.

Key points

Keep calm in an emergency.

Know how to ring the emergency services.

Think about doing a first-aid course yourself.

1. Hold the child over your knee and slap firmly between the child's shoulder blades. Get emergency help if the child's condition doesn't improve.

2. Get emergency help if the child is sick or sleepy after a bump to the head – they could have a head injury, which can be very dangerous.

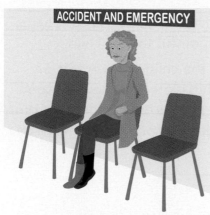

Activity

Make an information leaflet for new parents, giving details of how to contact the emergency services.

Com

3. Get emergency help and take the tablet bottle with you.

4. Comfort the child, and wash the graze with cold water. You may need to put a plaster on the graze (as long as the child is not allergic to plasters).

Always keep calm in an emergency. It upsets the child even more if you are panicking

Signs of ill health in children

Some children get what we call 'childhood illnesses'. Below are some examples of these illnesses. You may have had them yourself when you were younger.

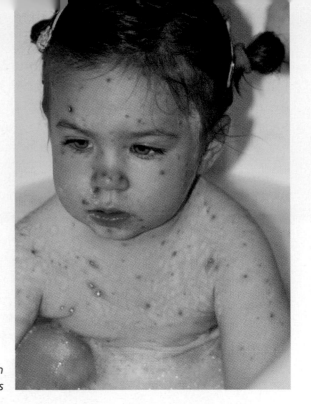

Chickenpox is a common childhood illness

Illness	Signs and symptoms	Treatment
Chickenpox	Groups of red spots with white centres that are very itchy. The child may also have a slight fever.	Use a soothing lotion (a chemist can advise), keep the child's nails clean, short and filed so they don't scratch.
Tonsillitis	A very sore throat – child can't swallow as it hurts a lot. Also gives earache and headache, and often a high temperature too.	Lots of comfort and drinks. A visit to the doctor is needed for antibiotics.
Ear infections	Earache, headache and often the child is sick. Child cries a lot.	Visit the doctor as soon as possible, as this is very painful for the child.
Diarrhoea and sickness	The child is always being sick and has very runny diarrhoea, a tummy ache and often a temperature.	Encourage the child to drink lots of cooled boiled water, as they can soon dehydrate. If it continues for more than 24 hours the child needs to be seen by a doctor.

Signs and symptoms

The following signs show that a child may be ill:

- flushed cheeks
- headache
- pale skin
- being sick

- diarrhoea
- whingeing
- crying
- won't eat

- coughing and sneezing
- very hot
- very sleepy.

Tips for looking after a child who is unwell

The parent or carer needs to:

- comfort and reassure the child
- make sure the child is comfortable (clean and dry)
- make sure the child has plenty to drink, but nothing icy cold
- make sure the child has quiet activities like reading or colouring-in to do
- make sure food is in small portions that look nice to eat
- keep the child's room not too hot or too cold
- spend plenty of time with the child.

Key points

Children who are not feeling well often just want their parents to sit and cuddle them. Parents can help by reading stories to them.

Activity

Write a suitable story for a 3-year-old child who is ill. Add pictures to the story. See if you can word-process your story.

Com ICT

A sick child needs more attention than usual

Accidents in the home and garden

Don't let children play in the loft

Bedroom dangers

- Pills left out
- Makeup
- Hair curlers that may be hot
- Bouncing on the beds and falling
- Windows need safety locks

Hall, stairs and landing

- No toys on stairs
- Use stair gates
- Watch young children on stairs

Bathroom dangers

- Don't leave children alone in the bath as they can drown
- Shaving equipment needs to be out of the way
- Hot water can scald
- Keep medicines and cleaning liquids in a locked cupboard

Living room/dining room

- Fireguards need to be in place
- Plug socket covers in the plugs
- Keep cigarettes and lighters out of the way
- Don't leave hot drinks about
- Check furniture for sharp edges

Kitchen

- Don't let children play on their own
- Lock cleaning equipment away
- Don't have pan handles over the front of the cooker
- Keep flexes, e.g. kettle flex, away from the edge of the worktop

Look at the rooms in the house opposite – in them are some causes of accidents in the home. Can you think of any more?

Many accidents can happen in the garden:

- garden tools left on the grass can cut or trip up
- poisonous plants, especially if they look like food, can make a child really poorly if eaten
- chemicals like weedkiller can make a child very sick
- washing lines and props (to hold the lines up) can cause children to trip
- uneven paths can lead to trips and falls
- ponds – children can easily fall in and drown
- make sure gates and fences are secure so children won't escape
- overflowing rubbish bins invite flies and wasps.

Watch out for hazards in the garden

Accidents outside the home

Outdoor hazards (out of the garden)

- Traffic can be a big problem. Teach children to cross the road in a safe place.
- Check that play equipment is safe before children play on it.
- Rubbish or overflowing bins – children need to learn not to touch other people's litter, and to put their own litter in the bin rather than dropping it on the ground. Wasps and other insects live around bins and could sting.
- Strangers – make sure you can see the children in your care at all times. Tell them they must not go anywhere with anyone they do not know.
- Dogs – encourage children not to go up to dogs or other animals, and especially ones they don't know, as they may get bitten. Take care to watch for dog mess, too.
- Watch children carefully near ponds and rivers – a child can drown even in very shallow water.

As parents and carers we need to think very carefully before we take babies and young children out anywhere.

Outings can be fun, but you must watch children carefully

A day trip to the beach needs careful planning!

Here is a list of some of the things you may need for a trip to the beach:

- pram or pushchair
- raincoat and wellingtons
- sandals and sunhats
- sun cream
- toys – beach ball and buckets and spades
- drink and something to eat
- changes of clothes
- extra nappies
- baby wipes (often washing facilities are not available – some people take a wet flannel instead of wipes)
- tissues or kitchen roll to clean up
- first-aid wipes
- reins for young children who want to walk.

The following hazards are especially important to watch out for with young children:

- sunburn – a child's skin is very sensitive to the sun and can quickly burn
- heatstroke – an illness caused by spending too long in the sun. Children are particularly vulnerable
- dehydration – an illness caused by not drinking enough fluids like water, milk or weak fruit juice.

Key points

There is a lot to think about before you take children out anywhere.

Activity

Write a letter to new parents, telling them what things they will need to take with them if they take their baby out for the day.

Com

The child's daily routine

Exercise

Why is exercise important?

- it improves balance and co-ordination
- it helps a child's lungs to develop
- it allows children to let off steam and have fun
- it allows children to play freely with others
- it increases the heart rate and circulation
- it helps strengthen bones
- it makes children hungry (gives them an appetite)
- it helps muscles to develop
- it keeps weight down.

Fresh air

It is important that children can go and play outside. If it is cold outside, but not raining, children should still go out to play, as long as they are well wrapped-up.

They may not stay outside very long, or sit down and play like they would on a nice sunny day, but fresh air is very important. Think how you would feel if you were shut inside all the time.

Some children love being outside and splashing in puddles with wellington boots on.

If they are suitably dressed, children can play outside in any weather

Being able to get fresh air and exercise depends on where you live. Children who live in the countryside or near a park or the beach have easier access to outdoor areas than children who live in tower blocks in a city or town.

Children who live in cities may have easier access to sports centres or swimming pools. These activities can be expensive, though, and need a lot of time from parents to take them there.

Key points

Always remember that young children should not go out by themselves as they could come to harm.

Activity

Using the Yellow Pages phone book, see if you can make a list of suitable places where parents could take their children near where you live.

Com

Your local sports centre may offer children's activity sessions

Washing hands and cleaning teeth

We have already discussed our own personal hygiene (how we take care of ourselves), and it is important that we teach children to take care of themselves too.

We need to be good role models because children copy us. For example, if children see us washing our hands after going to the toilet, they will wash their hands too.

Hand-washing

When we wash our hands we do it without thinking about the temperature of the water, how much soap to use, or how to dry our hands.

Young children don't wash their hands correctly unless they are shown how to. It's a good idea to show them how to wash their hands. You have to break the task of hand-washing into small steps.

It is important that as well as showing children how to wash their hands, you make sure they also dry their hands well – especially between their fingers. This is so they don't become sore.

Encourage children to use a nail brush to clean their nails. Fingernails should be cut by an adult, but you can encourage children to file their nails using an emery board.

Talking to young children about the task they are doing is a good way of practising communication skills.

Cleaning teeth

In our lifetime we will all have two sets of teeth. It is important that we look after our own teeth, because if we don't then we will end up with false teeth.

Young children need to be shown how to clean their own teeth properly, using their own child-sized toothbrush and gentle child's toothpaste. They should be strongly encouraged to do this.

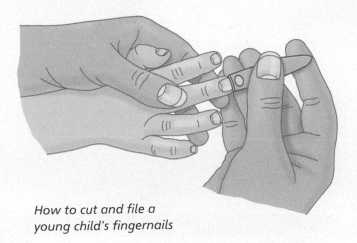

How to cut and file a young child's fingernails

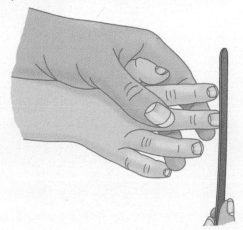

As soon as a baby's teeth begin to grow (at about 6 months) they should be gently brushed with a baby toothbrush.

Toddlers love doing things for themselves, but they often don't clean their teeth properly, and just chew their toothbrushes instead. Toddlers should be encouraged to clean their teeth after meals and before bedtime. Remember to use children's toothpaste as it is not as strong as adults' toothpaste.

Parents can be good role models and show children how to clean their teeth by brushing their teeth at the same time. Remember to praise the child for their attempt at cleaning their own teeth.

As children get older they still need encouragement to clean their teeth. Try to avoid sugary drinks and food with children of all ages, as this can cause teeth to decay (rot and grow holes).

Key points

Children need encouragement and praise as they start to become independent and do more for themselves.

Parents and carers still need to remind young children how to do things like cleaning their teeth.

Activity

Design a poster with instructions for either hand-washing or teeth-cleaning – make it suitable for young children (lots of pictures and colours).

Com

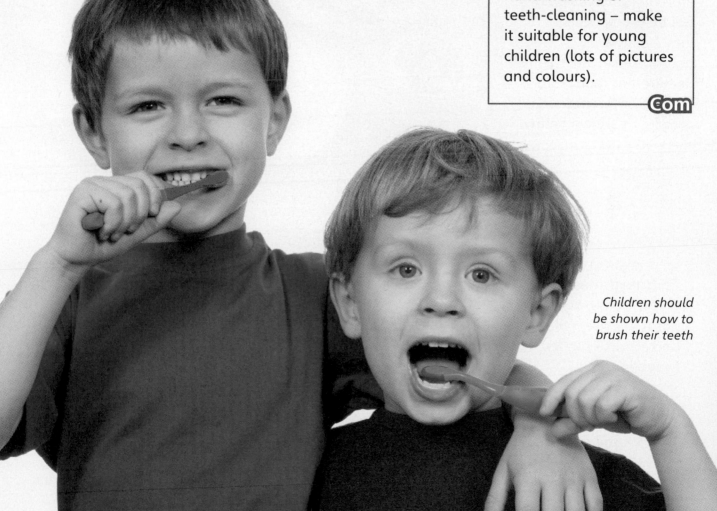

Children should be shown how to brush their teeth

A healthy diet for children

It is very important that young children eat well. Parents and carers need to provide meals that contain many different types of foods to make sure that they get the full range of nutrients (essential things for a healthy body). Children need to eat what we call a balanced diet.

Why do we need a balanced diet?

If we ate chips for every meal, we would not be eating a balanced diet. If we ate just salad – lettuce, tomatoes and cucumber – although it would be more healthy, it would not be a balanced diet. To have a balanced diet we need to eat food from the five different food groups, as shown below.

Children need a balanced diet

Carbohydrates
Bread, pasta, noodles, potatoes, rice, pulses and natural sugars found in fruit

Food can be broken down into five different nutrient groups

Protein
Meat, eggs, beans, fish, and dairy produce, such as cheese

Vitamins
Carrots, milk, bread, cereals, green leafy vegetables and fruit

Fat
Butter, margarine and vegetable oils, fatty foods like burgers

Minerals
Red meat, broccoli, spinach, milk, yoghurt and egg yolks

The table below shows you why the body needs these different nutrients and in which foods they can be found.

Nutrient group	Why the body needs it	Food example
Protein	For growth and repair of the cells and tissues in the body	Meat, fish, milk
Carbohydrates	For energy that is to be used quickly	Potatoes, pasta
Fats	For energy that can be stored and provide warmth for the body	Butter, margarine and some meats
Vitamins	To help control body systems such as circulation of the blood	Cereals, green leafy vegetables like spinach
Minerals	To help control body systems such as blood cells and for growth and repair	Red meat, egg yolks

Young children need encouragement to try out new foods, so introduce things slowly and give them lots of praise if they have a taste.

Key points

Remember to be a good role model as a parent/carer at meal times, as children will copy you. If you put your knife into your mouth, children will do the same.

Praise good table manners at mealtimes.

Activity

Using food magazines, cut out pictures and drawings of suitable food for children, and design a menu for two children's meals. This looks great stuck on a paper plate.

Com

Children need smaller portions than adults and need to have their food presented nicely

Clothing for babies and young children

We all like babies and children to look nice. However, there are important things to remember when dressing babies and children.

Babies

- Babies need clothes that fit them properly. Clothes that are too small don't allow babies to move and can easily cut into the skin if too tight.

- Babies need layers of clothing that can be easily taken off or added if they become too hot or cold, as they cannot control their body temperature.

- Babies can be very messy, so clothes need to be easily washed and dried.

- Because babies wear nappies, they need to have clothes that allow for easy nappy changes for parents and carers to manage.

- When outside, babies should wear hats: a sunhat to protect from the sun and a hat to keep their head warm in cold weather.

- Babies don't really need shoes until they can walk. Socks and the feet of baby-grows must be big enough not to squash the baby's feet.

The different clothes a new baby needs

A baby dressed for summer   *A baby dressed for winter*

Young children

There are many different types of clothes for babies and children. Sometimes we may buy clothes that are not suitable for young children.

A child who is toilet training would be better to wear clothes with poppers or press studs that can be removed quickly, rather than clothes with buttons, which might be harder to manage.

Clothes must not be too tight or too loose for children. Cotton material is best for them as it allows their skin to breathe.

Children need to wear clothes that are comfortable and suitable for the weather and their activity. They shouldn't wear sandals in the snow or a thick coat in hot weather. Clothes need to be tough enough to survive children's rough and tumble types of play. Best clothes are no good for messy play activities. Children should be encouraged to wear aprons, especially for painting and gluing activities.

Clothes should be easy to wash, as children can quickly get dirty when playing.

Key points

Clothes for babies and young children must be suitable for what they are doing.

Young children need to have spare clothes with them as they may have accidents if they can't get to the toilet in time.

Activity

Using clothes catalogues, choose winter and summer clothes for a young child. Choose for either a boy or a girl. Remember to include pants, vests, shorts, trousers, skirts, hats, coats, sandals and shoes and so on.

Rest and sleep

It is important that babies and children get plenty of rest and sleep, as this is when their bodies can grow and develop.

Parents and carers need to understand the common signs of tiredness in babies and children.

Babies need lots of sleep – in fact most of their time is spent asleep, and they only wake up to be fed or have their nappy changed.

Toddlers and young children need to have a good night's sleep as they are very active in the daytime. Many will still need a nap in the afternoon too.

A quiet activity like story-telling is a good way to encourage rest. Often the child (and sometimes the parent) will fall asleep before the end of the story.

Other activities for quiet rest times are:
- looking at pictures in books – like nursery rhymes
- listening to a story tape or music playing quietly
- watching a children's video or DVD
- doing a puzzle
- drawing a picture.

Some children don't think they need a nap in the daytime as they don't feel tired. They may not want to go to bed, but will sit quietly with you for a story or to watch a children's TV programme.

Resting is good as it helps children to relax, especially after playing outside in the fresh air. Sometimes children can become overtired – a child who is overtired may stop behaving as they should – and resting can prevent this.

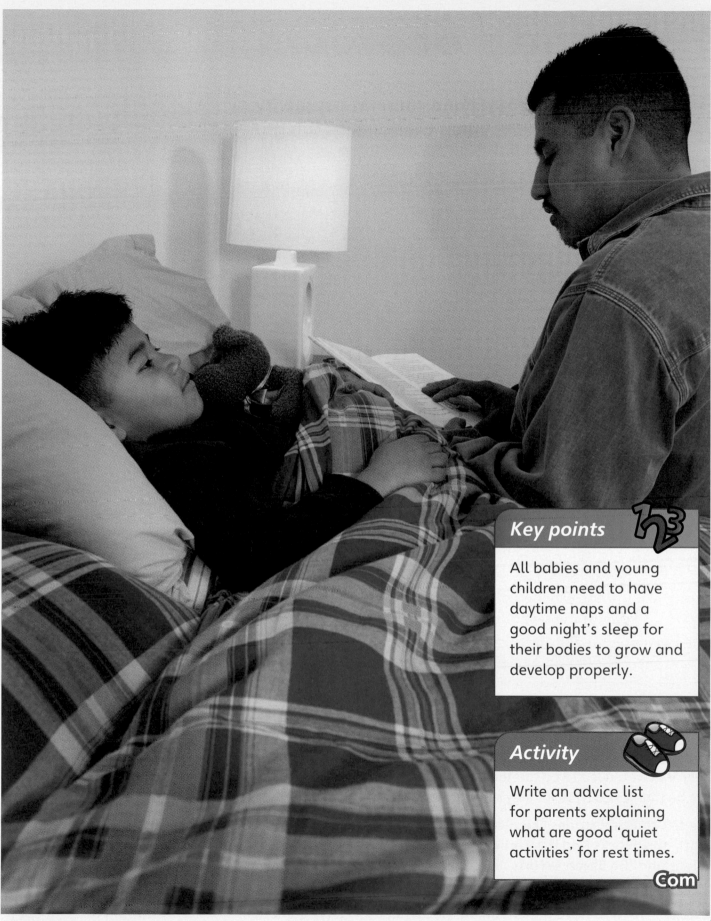

Key points

All babies and young children need to have daytime naps and a good night's sleep for their bodies to grow and develop properly.

Activity

Write an advice list for parents explaining what are good 'quiet activities' for rest times.

Com

A tired child is usually happy to lie quietly for a story

The child's bedroom

It is important to think carefully about the layout of a child's bedroom – what do we need to think about?

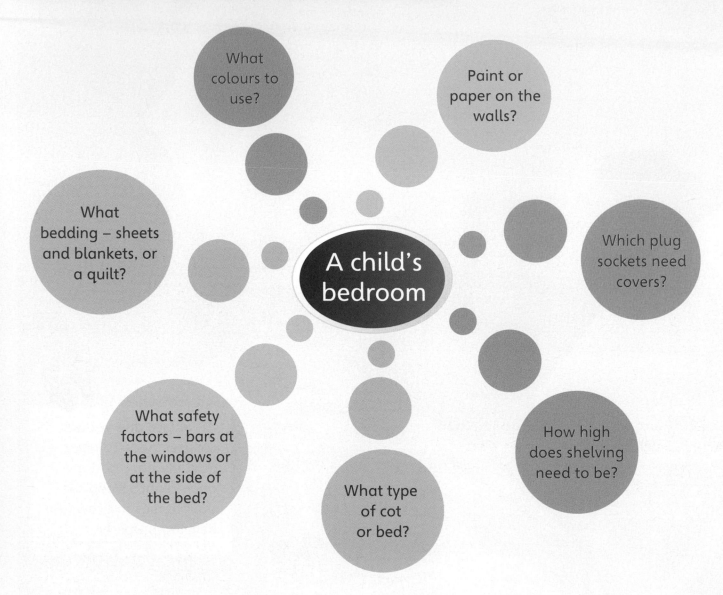

What colours to use?

Paint or paper on the walls?

What bedding – sheets and blankets, or a quilt?

A child's bedroom

Which plug sockets need covers?

What safety factors – bars at the windows or at the side of the bed?

What type of cot or bed?

How high does shelving need to be?

When choosing wallpaper or pictures for a child's bedroom, you need to be careful that the child will not be frightened by what they see in the pictures.

We tell children stories like the 'Three Little Pigs', 'Goldilocks and the Three Bears', or 'Snow White and the Seven Dwarfs', but a very young child may think these stories are real.

Curtains need to have a good lining material, otherwise the sun will keep the child awake late on summer evenings and wake them very early in the morning.

Shelving and cupboard space are important in a child's room. Shelving shouldn't be too high as a child may be encouraged to climb for a toy or book on a high shelf.

Children should be encouraged to put heavy toys and books onto a bottom shelf.

Children need plenty of sleep – if their curtains are too thin, they are likely to wake early

Children should also be encouraged to put toys away once they have finished playing with them. This encourages them to become tidy, and understand that things like clothes and toys need to be put away tidily.

Key points

Children's bedrooms should be calm, tidy places if they are to encourage children to rest and sleep.

Don't have anything on the walls that may frighten a child.

Activity

Using shop catalogues, scissors and glue, design a child's bedroom for a boy or a girl. Look at the diagram on page 56 for the areas you need to think about.

AoN

Bedtime routines

Bathtime

Children need to have a routine before they go to bed (a routine is something that is the same or similar every time) so that they know what to do and what is expected to happen. And remember that bathtimes should be fun!

Most bedtimes start with bathtime. It is important to remember that extra care needs to be taken at bathtime as it can be a dangerous time for young children and babies.

You should always remember to:

- stay with babies and young children at bathtime. **Never** leave them while you answer the phone or the door – a child can easily drown, even in shallow water

- have everything that you need ready before the child gets into the bath so you don't have to leave the child alone

- put the cold water into the bath before the hot, as sometimes children jump into the bath before you have said it is ready, and if you have put hot water in first it is very easy for the child to get scalded

- use children's bubble bath and shampoo – however, you still need to be careful as these can sting a child's eyes

- use a safety mat in the bottom of the bath, and don't overfill the bath with toys

- make sure the child is properly dry after the bath, especially between their fingers and toes.

Never leave a child alone in the bath

Feeding before bedtime

Babies often need a feed before bedtime. Remember not to leave a young baby on its own with a bottle because it may choke.

Baby bottles that are full of juice are also a bad idea because the sugar in the juice can rot a child's teeth. Water or milk are good drinks at bedtime.

Sometimes a young child has a plain biscuit with a drink of milk. We often call this last snack 'supper'.

Remember that children need to clean their teeth before they go to bed. A visit to the toilet followed by washing hands is a good idea too.

Children may need a quiet activity before they go to bed to help them settle down. A bedtime story is ideal – nothing that will scare the child, though.

Many children are frightened of the dark so using a night light is a good idea. There are many different night lights available.

Key points

Children need to follow a bedtime routine so that they know what is happening.

Activity

Design a poster of safe tips for bathtime for parents. You could try doing this on a computer.

Com ICT

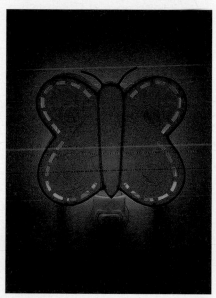

A night light will help to reassure a child who is afraid of the dark

Cereal and milk is good at bedtime

Bedtime blues

Reasons why a child may not want to go to bed

Sometimes a child doesn't want to go to bed, even though he or she is used to a bedtime routine. This could be because the child:

- is frightened of the dark
- does not feel tired
- wants to stay up and play with an older brother or sister
- is frightened of something they have seen on the television
- is frightened of something they have heard, for example a ghost story
- wants to spend time with a parent who has been working late
- wants to watch a favourite TV programme that is on later than usual
- knows you have visitors coming and wants to see them
- has too many distractions in the bedroom with all their toys about.

Children can sometimes be afraid of imaginary (not real) monsters and ghosts. It can be difficult for children to understand that they are not real.

To an adult it may seem a silly reason, but the child needs you to understand, support and reassure them rather than be cross.

Being a responsible parent/carer means you make sure you know what TV and storybooks children have access to before bedtime.

What to do when a child doesn't want to go to bed

It can be very difficult when a child doesn't want to go to bed. It can be easy for parents and carers to get cross with the child and shout at them.

Children can be frightened by dreams and need reassurance

If a child refuses to go to bed it is important that you:

- stick with the bedtime routine – if you don't, the child might continue to play up at bedtime
- stay calm – shouting is not an effective way of dealing with the child. Often all it does is make the child shout back at you
- try to compromise with the child – it is better to try and persuade the child to go to bed by offering something in return – maybe the child can stay up a little later at the weekend

Shouting is not an effective way of dealing with a child who doesn't want to go to bed

Praise

Once the child does as he/she is asked, you need to praise and encourage this positive behaviour at bedtime as this is what you want to see again.

Bedtime reward chart

A good way of keeping a check on behaviour at bedtime is to use a star chart or a smiley face chart and give a reward after a period of good behaviour.

Key points

Always praise the kind of behaviour you want to see repeated – if a child is good at going to bed, then praise them.

Activity

Design your own reward chart. Can you think of something different to the two examples above?

AoN

A star chart

A smiley face chart

M	T	W	T	F	S	S	or	M	T	W	T	F	S	S
☆	☆	☆	☆	☆	☆	☆		☺	☺	☺	☺	☺	☺	☺

Sleep safe

Once babies or children are in bed, it is important that they stay safe. Never go out and leave babies or young children asleep in bed alone in the house. You should choose babysitters carefully as they have to be responsible for the welfare and safety of very vulnerable children.

Here are some safe sleeping tips for babies and toddlers.

Babies

- The bedroom needs to be at the right temperature – about 18 degrees centigrade – not too hot or too cold. Keep babies out of the way of draughts (cold air).

- Babies need to be placed on their backs at the bottom of the cot. Check that the covers are not over the baby's face.

- Don't leave a baby with a bottle in case the baby chokes.

Never leave a sleeping baby or child alone in the house

Toddlers and young children

Toddlers and young children don't always want to go to bed when you tell them it is bedtime!

- Have a quiet time before bedtime – choose quiet activities that will help to set the scene for rest.
- Keep to the set routine every night so the child starts to expect what is going to happen.
- Before bed you need to check that the sleeping area is safe, as children of this age don't stay in their bed but tend to get out to play with their toys.

Once the babies or children are fast asleep you should check on them from time to time. Some children need to be lifted up when you go to bed and taken to the toilet again.

You must be very quiet when you check on children while they are asleep. If you make too much noise you could wake them up and they will be ready to play again – while you want to go to bed!

Children often wet the bed at night – this is usually because they sleep so heavily they don't realise they need the toilet until it is too late. Although this is inconvenient for you, as you have to change the bed, the child cannot help it. Shouting at the child will not help. Children eventually grow out of this. In the meantime, you can get plastic sheeting to protect the mattress, and night-care pants for children can help.

Summary of Unit 2

- Personal hygiene is important when you are looking after young children.
- Keep calm in an emergency: reassure the child that they will be OK, and comfort them in a calm voice.
- Parents and carers need to look out for dangers as children don't yet understand how to.
- You need to plan before taking children on an outing.
- Don't leave young children on their own – they may come to harm.
- Encourage children to do things for themselves (where safe).
- Be a good role model for children.
- Children's clothes must be suitable for their level of development and the activity.
- Babies and young children need plenty of sleep and naps to recharge their energy levels.
- A child's bedroom should be a happy place to be.
- Bedtime routines are very important for children.
- Praise good bedtime behaviour.
- Don't leave babies and young children alone in the house at night – or at any time.

Unit 3 Playing and learning in the home

Introduction

This unit is all about how babies and children learn through play. You will learn about:

- different types of play
- stages of play
- how to choose toys
- toys for babies
- toy safety
- making household items suitable for play
- natural materials
- routines for playtime
- choosing television and DVDs for young children
- the role of the parent or carer during play
- valuing children – self-esteem
- good communication
- good role model
- books and poems
- managing children's behaviour
- play provision for young children.

Glossary

Here are some of the words you will meet in this unit. Some of them may be new to you:

- **Associative play** – children are beginning to play together

- **Communicate** – we communicate with each other to pass on information

- **Confidence** – we gain 'confidence' to do things, e.g. to read aloud in class

- **Co-operative play** – children are beginning to plan for play

- **Crèche** – where children are cared for while parents are at work

- **Development** – the way children learn to use their bodies and gain skills

- **Imagination** – where children pretend to be someone or something else

- **Natural materials** – objects that are part of nature, such as trees or water

- **Open questions** – questions that need more than 'yes' or 'no' as the answer

- **Parallel play** – where children are playing next to each other but not sharing toys or talking

- **Peer group** – children in the same group, of a similar age

- **Positive reinforcement** – praising good behaviour that we want to see repeated

- **Self-esteem** – how you feel about yourself

- **Solitary play** – when a child plays on its own

- **Spectator play** – when a child watches other children play

- **Statutory** – a rule set by the government

- **Texture** – how things feel

The importance of play

**Children learn through play. Play is fun.
Sometimes people say that play is children's work.**

Play

Young children spend most of their waking time playing. They move from one toy to another, one activity to another. Each child has different levels of concentration – how long they stay with one toy or activity. Some children enjoy playing in the sand, some like to do craft activities, and some children like to sit quietly with books.

Why play is important to babies and young children

Babies and children love to play with toys. They sometimes play with one toy for a long time, or they may play with lots of different toys. Babies often lie in their cots and watch a mobile above them. They 'coo' and 'babble' to the mobile, they point to the toys on the mobile.

Concepts like time, numbers and shapes, for example by counting cups in the home corner.

To practise different skills like building and writing, for example through playing with bricks and using the writing table.

Through play children learn

To have fun with others, to learn to share and how to communicate with other children.

To explore and experiment, to try, fail and try again, for example when doing a jigsaw, trying each piece until they find the right one.

Some babies have activity centres fixed to the sides of their cots. They soon learn to press the button to make a bell ring – or shake the rattle.

As babies grow into toddlers, they play with different toys. Most young children love bricks, or 'construction play'. Duplo is a good way for children to start to develop skills. An adult can help by repeating the names of the colours of the bricks, and helping children learn to count. Questions such as 'How many red bricks do you have?' are a good way to introduce numbers.

Even young babies need to have something to interest them

Key points

All children need the freedom to play and learn at their own speed in a safe environment.

Children need to play with toys that are suitable for their age.

Activity

1 Think about the toys you had as a child, and what skills you gained from these toys – make a list.

2 Using either the Internet or a toy catalogue, choose a young child's toy you like. Glue the picture into the middle of a piece of paper and write around the picture (like a spider diagram) what a young child could learn from this toy.

ICT

Types of play

There are many different types of play.

Type of play	Explanation	Picture
Mastery play	This is where babies and very young children do the same thing over and over again until they 'master' it – or do it correctly. They often play with the toy once they have mastered it.	
Discovery play	This is when children begin to find out about the world around them, for example discovering the shape, size, colour and texture of different objects.	
Creative play	This is when a child expresses his or her own thoughts and feelings to make something unique, such as a painting or drawing.	
Social play	This is when children play together, learning to share and take turns. Social play teaches children what is the right/acceptable kind of behaviour towards others.	
Pretend play	This is when children are using their imagination to pretend they are something or someone else.	

Physical play	Children develop their muscle skills through play. **Fine manipulative** – using fingers to thread beads or hold a paintbrush. **Gross motor** – play using large muscles as in running, jumping, riding a bike.	
Construction play	This is when children use bricks, model materials, such as cereal boxes, or Lego to construct something.	

Play helps children to develop new skills:

- Physical skills   →   Hand-to-eye co-ordination
                                 Co-ordination and balance

- Social skills   →   Sharing and taking turns
                                 Co-operating with others
                                 Communicating with others
                                 Making friends

- Intellectual skills → Developing language skills
                                 Learning about the outside world
                                 Developing concentration skills
                                 Learning how to predict
                                 Developing imagination
                                 Learning to experiment and test
                                 Developing creativity

- Emotional skills   →   Having freedom to play
                                 Beginning to control feelings
                                 Learning good behaviour
                                 Developing confidence
                                 Developing independence
                                 Acting out roles from real life

Key points

An activity can include different types of play: creating a picture needs hand-to-eye co-ordination and can include discovery play, such as mixing blue and yellow paint to make green paint.

Activity

1 Think of two activities and write about the different types of play involved in each one.

2 Make a list of equipment you would need for each activity. Plan for four children – so you may need four paintbrushes, for example.

Stages of play

Between the ages of 1 and 5, children change in the way they play, from playing on their own to being able to organise and plan their play with other children. Most children will pass through the following stages.

Solitary play

This is when a child is playing by itself. Usually up to the age of 2 years, children are not interested in playing with other children.

Parallel play

This is when two children are playing next to each other, but not with each other. Each child has their own toy; the children do not share or talk to each other.

Looking on (spectator play)

This is where a child stands 'outside' the play area, watching what is going on. The child is not confident enough to join in with the play.

Very young children are not ready to play with other children, but are happy to play by themselves

A child will often watch others playing before joining in

Associative play

This is when children begin to play together, usually from the age of 3 years. Children often copy what they see others doing.

Co-operative play

This kind of play happens when children have been playing together for a while. They now start planning for playing together, often with complicated rules.

Preventing accidents

There are many places where you can buy toys for children. Toyshops, supermarkets, markets, catalogue shops, and so on. We have to take a lot of care when choosing toys for children under 4 years old.

Choosing suitable toys for children

Make sure the toy will last a long time.

Make sure the toy doesn't have sharp or small parts.

Make sure the toy can be shared with other children.

Make sure toys are suitable for the child's age.

When buying toys you should

Make sure the toy can be easily cleaned.

Make sure the toy can be shared with other children.

Make sure the toy is good value – that the child will want to play with it more than once.

Make sure the toy can be easily stored.

Babies explore toys by putting everything in their mouths, so great care must be taken when choosing toys for babies. Babies need to have clean toys as they can easily become ill.

All new toys and equipment should carry a safety mark. You must also follow the manufacturer's instructions when giving toys to babies and young children.

Checking old toys and equipment

Checking toys and equipment can help to prevent accidents. If toys are old or have been played with a lot they may have started to come apart. This sometimes leads to sharp edges or tiny pieces that a young child could swallow. If large equipment such as slides, swings or climbing frames start coming apart, this could result in a nasty fall.

Cleaning toys and equipment

To prevent children becoming ill from putting dirty toys in their mouths, you should regularly clean toys and equipment with a weak solution of disinfectant. This helps to kill any bacteria or germs on the toys. Always make sure toys are well rinsed and dried before giving them to young children.

Some of the safety marks you may see on toys or other safety related products

Key points
Always choose toys very carefully for babies and young children – if you don't, the toys could hurt them.

Activity
Design a safety poster showing parents what they should remember when buying toys or cleaning and checking toys that have been bought.

Com

Toys for age and stage of development

It is important that toys are suitable for the age and development of the child. Remember how young children explore new things. They put things in their mouths, so you have to be careful of small pieces.

For example, young children shouldn't have Lego; it has small parts and a child may choke if they put small parts in their mouth. Duplo bricks are much safer.

Treasure baskets

For babies from 6 months a treasure basket is a good activity. A variety of safe toys and other suitable objects can be put in a basket for a baby to explore.

Some things you could put in a treasure basket

Babies and young children should never be left alone when playing; an adult should stay close by, quietly talking to the baby/toddler.

Adapting household items for play activities

You don't always have to buy toys for young children. Sometimes they like to play with household objects like pans and spoons.

Don't let children play with anything made from glass. Anything that is sharp or has small parts is dangerous.

Children are learning about their environment all the time, often asking questions about what you are doing and why. Children like to help in the house, so try to let them take part in everyday routines.

Remember to be sensitive when including children in household chores. Think about the child's ability and introduce tasks slowly. Try and make tasks into a game, for example sorting socks into colours and pairs.

Always praise the child for helping, don't criticise them for being too slow or getting things wrong: children need to feel that they are helping.

Key points

Remember that children will copy what you do – so think about the things that you do.

Activity

1 Can you think of three other 'jobs' at home that children can help with?

2 What safety things must you think about when children are helping in the home?

Com

Natural and manufactured materials

Natural materials are objects like stones and wood, that grow and occur as part of nature. Manufactured materials are things like plastic and cardboard, that are produced using heat, machines or chemicals.

By playing with natural materials a young child can discover much about the world around them. Playing with sand and shells can teach children about the textures of the seashore. Playing with wood (that has been sanded down, so that there are no sharp edges) gives children a chance to explore a natural material.

Sometimes natural materials need to be put together to make play equipment. Playing with home-made play dough is a good activity for young children. The recipe opposite shows you how to make your own play dough.

Play dough

2 cups flour
2 cups water
1 cup salt
1 spoon oil
1 spoon food colouring

1. Put all the ingredients into a pan.
2. Cook over a medium heat, stirring all the time until the mixture comes away from the sides of the pan.
3. When rolling out the dough, don't use extra flour, as this will make it go mouldy.
4. Store the play dough in a sealed container in the fridge.

Play dough is a great activity for children to explore; fine manipulative skills are used in rolling, squeezing and pressing the dough. Creative and imaginative skills are used in deciding what to make; different colours help children learn names of colours.

Play dough lets children use their hands and their imagination

How much sand does the truck hold?

Children learn useful skills through play

Some ways children learn from natural and manufactured materials

Physical

- Hand-to-eye co-ordination
- Fine manipulative skills in pouring.

Intellectual / cognitive

- New concepts – half-full/half-empty, sinking and floating
- Learn about volume and capacity (how much sand in a bucket?)
- Develops concentration skills
- Encourages thought processes = what to do.

Language

- Talking to each other
- Learning new words = describing things.

Emotional

Most children enjoy playing in the sand tray: it's non-threatening, not right or wrong; they can repeat the same task over and over again.

Social

- Learning to share equipment
- Learning what is acceptable behaviour.

Adults' role

Adults must supervise when children are playing with natural materials. Outside sandpits need to be kept covered between playtimes as cats may use the sand pit as a toilet.

Key points

Children may spend a long time playing in a sand pit – filling a bucket and emptying it again. Just because there is no finished product, like a painting, doesn't mean they haven't learned anything.

Activity

1 List the different things you can add to a sand or water tray.

2 Make some play dough. How does playing with the dough make you feel?

Com AoN

Choosing television programmes and DVDs for children

We all have our favourite programmes on the television, from football to soaps, from the news to comedy programmes. Children are the same.

It is important when we let children watch television that the programmes are suitable for their age. Children will enjoy programmes and DVDs they can learn from and that are easy to understand.

Most children like, and learn from, programmes such as *Dora the Explorer* or *Charlie and Lola*, with friendly presenters who talk to children in the correct way.

Watching a TV programme can be a chance to share some quiet time together

Suitability of TV or DVDs for children

It is important to be clear about which TV programmes and DVDs are not suitable for children.

A violent or scary programme will probably upset the child, and may lead to bad dreams or nightmares.

Adult programmes may contain fighting, swearing or scenes of a sexual nature. Children like to copy what they see, so it is important that they watch only what is suitable for their age.

Repeatedly watching the same DVD may become dull, although some children may have a favourite programme that they like to watch regularly.

If programmes are too difficult for children to understand, they may become bored.

Benefits of watching TV or DVDs for children

Watching television or a DVD can give children some time to rest. As a parent or carer it could mean you spend some time quietly together.

Talking about the programme you have watched can encourage communication skills. Asking open-ended questions (questions that need more than a 'yes' or 'no' answer) is good because it encourages the child to think of an answer.

A good question could be: 'Which part of the programme did you like?', rather than 'Did you like that?'

Some programmes encourage children to sing along or dance to the tunes. Adult participation is good – this kind of activity encourages a child to keep fit.

Key points

Young children should not be left to watch television for long periods of time. They need to do other activities too. Young children need to be allowed to play and have exercise and fresh air to help them develop into healthy children.

Activity

1 Watch two children's TV programmes and make a list of the different things children could learn from watching them, for example 'new songs' if it is a children's music show.

2 Think about your favourite programme. Make a scrapbook of the characters and write your own story for the programme. What would you like to happen to the characters?

Com

The role of the parent during play

Safety

Being a parent or carer is probably one of the hardest jobs to do. One of the most important parts of this job is to keep babies and children safe, especially when they are playing, as they are unable to think about their own safety.

We have already talked about toy safety in this section, about making sure that toys have a safety mark and are suitable for the children's age and stage of development.

It is also important that you watch children while they are playing – in childcare we call this supervising children's play.

This means you have to check the areas where the children are playing to make sure they are safe. Below are some examples of how to make sure places are safe for children to play, both inside and outside the home.

Inside the house

All plug sockets need to have covers to stop children putting their fingers into the holes in the socket.

A stair gate can keep children away from danger

Safety covers stop children putting their fingers into electric sockets

Children like to explore and may decide to climb stairs or go into rooms they shouldn't. Using a stair gate can prevent children getting into danger.

The use of fireguards and radiator guards is important to stop children getting burnt. Children like fires and they don't understand how dangerous it is if they go near one.

Outside in the garden

Children love playing in a sandpit. Sand should be children's play sand – sometimes called 'silver sand'. This is much better than building sand, which is sharp and will stain children's clothes. Adults must make sure that children learn not to throw sand as it may get into someone's eyes.

Adults should check large outside play equipment often, as children may cause some of the parts to come loose. The equipment must be safe for the children to play on – not too big or too high for them to climb. Adults must supervise when young children are playing on such equipment.

Key points

Babies and young children need parents and carers to look out for their safety when playing indoors or in the garden.

Activity

Make a list of the dangers that children might not be aware of when they are playing: a) indoors, b) in the garden.

Com

Children love to climb and swing, but an adult must check that the equipment is safe

Helping a child to feel valued

It is important that parents and carers help a child to feel valued. 'Valued' means loved, wanted and appreciated.

Children need to feel good about themselves. When you feel good about who you are, then you have a good sense of self-esteem.

Think about what makes you feel good about yourself. It might be that your tutor has said your work was excellent, or a friend says they like your new haircut.

A good sense of self-esteem is important in life: if you do not feel good about who you are, it's very hard to enjoy what you do. It can also make it hard to make friends because when you don't like who you are, you think other people won't like you either.

Self-esteem

Children who grow up with supportive adults who love, encourage, praise and care for them constantly have high self-esteem. This gives them confidence to face new people and situations.

Children need adults to take an interest in them

Children who are told they are stupid, or who are not praised when they have tried to do something new, who are ignored and not listened to, tend to have low self-esteem and little confidence.

It is very important that parents and carers take time to talk and listen to young children. This shows that you are interested in what they think and feel.

This makes a child feel valued and special and that they deserve your attention.

Activity

1 List five things that give you high self-esteem, such as praise.

2 List five things that can make you have low self-esteem, such as being told you are stupid.

Com

Key points

If you act in a positive way towards children, they will feel their efforts are valued – this leads to high self-esteem. Children who are always criticised may feel they are no good at anything and have low self-esteem.

Children respond well to attention from an adult

Good communications

For children to feel valued (and have high self-esteem) it is important that we listen to what they say. This sounds very easy to do, but to really listen to someone you need to give them your undivided attention.

'Listening' does not mean:

- watching television at the same time
- being distracted while a child is talking to you
- telling the child to hurry up
- yawning while the child is talking.

When you are really listening to a child it is not only the words you hear – it is how the child speaks to you. You may notice their tone of voice, their facial expression and their body posture.

These things tell you how a child is feeling. This can help when a young child is not sure how to put thoughts into words. Children often want to talk to you when you are busy, on the phone or talking to someone else.

Different ways we communicate:

- body language and gestures – using hands, arms, face, eyes and body to get a message across to someone
- sign language – a language used by children and adults with hearing impairments
- Braille – a way of writing for people who are blind.

Open and closed questions

One way we can show children we are listening to them is by asking open questions. These are questions that need more than a 'yes' or 'no' answer, and that require the child to say more about how they feel or what they think. This gives children a chance to say more about their experiences.

Other ways of communicating

Show that you are interested in what the child has to say

Open questions tell a child that you are interested in what they have to say.

Closed questions don't encourage a child to talk about what is going on – closed questions make it harder to speak to you.

Being a good role model

It is important that adults are good role models, showing children that we listen to them encourages them to listen to others.

Adults should:

- speak clearly
- use words children can understand
- use good eye contact
- use good manners ('please'/'thank you')
- not use bad language
- be polite and respectful.

Key points

Giving a child a chance to talk increases confidence and self-esteem.

Talking to a child politely means they will talk to you in the same way.

Activity

Think about all the different ways we communicate, for example, with text messages. Design a poster showing all the different types you can find.

Com

Enjoying books and poems

A good way of encouraging children to learn new words is by helping them to read books, look at pictures and talk about what they see.

There are many wonderful books available for children of all ages. Listening to stories and poems helps to develop a child's imagination.

Factual books are about real life and can teach children about the world around them.

Babies enjoy picture books – ones with bright colours and made from thick board are the best. Very young children like 'pop-up' books and 'touchy-feely' books, especially if they can take part.

Children can enjoy books from a very early age

Young children enjoy listening to simple stories, often over and over again. Books with little writing and bold pictures are best.

Looking at the words in the book while the adult reads the story aloud helps the child to learn different word sounds.

Young children also love counting books, nursery rhymes and poems.

Nursery rhymes

Nursery rhymes are a good way for children to learn language. They help children learn new words through rhythm and rhyming sounds. Below are some favourite nursery rhymes.

Listening to stories helps to develop a child's imagination

Incy Wincy Spider

Incy wincy spider climbed up the water spout.
(*Move your hands like a spider climbing up into the air.*)
Down came the rain and washed poor incy out.
(*Wiggle your fingers as you move your hands to look like rain.*)
Out came the sunshine and dried up all the rain,
(*Spread your fingers as you move your hands upwards*
and outwards to look like the sun.)
So incy wincy spider climbed up the spout again!
(*Move your hands like a spider climbing up into the air again.*)

Humpty Dumpty

Humpty Dumpty sat on a wall.
Humpty Dumpty had a great fall.
All the king's horses and all the king's men
Couldn't put Humpty together again!

Hickory Dickory Dock

Hickory dickory dock,
The mouse ran up the clock.
The clock struck one,
The mouse ran down.
Hickory dickory dock.

Children really like rhymes that involve their hands; they often learn the hand movements before the words.

Key points

Short stories with colourful pictures are wonderful in supporting new language development.

Activity

1 Think of your favourite story from when you were young – see if you can use the computer and type it out. Include a picture.

2 Choose your favourite rhyme and write it down. See if you can draw hand movements.

Com

Rhymes like 'Incy Wincy Spider' are good with hand movements

Good behaviour

'Behaviour' is the way we act and the way we speak to others. Children need to learn to speak and act in a way that is polite and acceptable to others.

Good behaviour means thinking about other people's needs as well as our own.

To be good means you:

- listen to others
- share and take turns
- are helpful and work together (co-operate)
- are polite and remember to say 'please' and 'thank you'
- look after your own things and other people's property.

Stages of learning good behaviour

Children have to learn how to behave. It is important that we understand that young children are not able to follow the same behaviour rules as we can.

At 1–2 years of age, children do not understand that toys may belong to others, and want everything.

At 2–3 years of age, children easily get cross and may have a tantrum when they cannot get their own way. They don't like sharing toys or adult time. Praising them lots when they are good helps them to get better at sharing.

At 4–5 years of age: children should now be playing nicely together (although squabbles still happen) they are beginning to plan for their play and follow simple rules. They can get very excited and noisy when playing.

Parents and carers need to be careful not to expect too much from young children. A 2-year-old will not understand why they can run and shout in the park, yet get told off if they do the same in the supermarket.

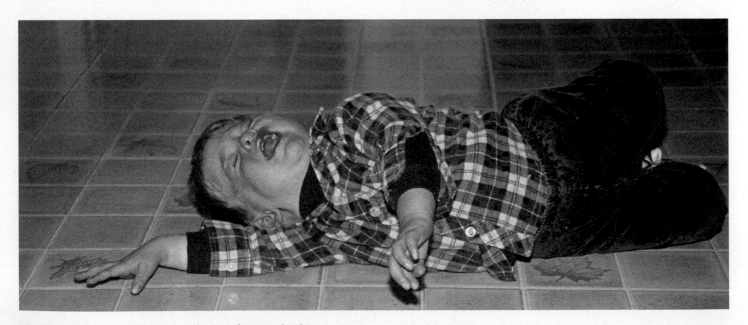

Young children can find it hard to understand rules

It is important that we praise good behaviour, as it is the behaviour we want to see again. Adults need to be good role models when teaching children about good behaviour, otherwise it can confuse the children. For example, children will be confused if they have to take off their shoes in the house and adults don't.

Stopping bad behaviour

There are different ways in which we can stop unacceptable behaviour:

- praise good behaviour
- make sure children understand the rules of games
- make sure there are enough toys to go around
- ignore bad behaviour (as long as no one is going to get hurt)
- try and get the child to play with something else
- set suitable rules and explain them, such as 'No running down the slide because you may get hurt'.

Key points

It's important that children are at the right age to understand the rules you make.

Always praise good behaviour as this is the kind of behaviour we want to see again.

Remember to be a good role model – don't shout at the children to stop shouting!

Activity

Design a poster showing what is acceptable (good) behaviour for people of your own age.

Com

Children learn by following the example of adults

Different types of play provision

There are three main categories (types) of play provision that you can use for young children.

Statutory

A statutory service is one that is provided by the government and funded by the taxes that we pay in our wages.

Nursery schools are called maintained nursery schools. They offer full-time or part-time places for children from 3 to 5 years of age.

Some primary schools have a nursery class, often in a separate building with teachers and nursery nurses looking after and teaching the children.

Many areas now have Children's Centres that provide day care for under-5s. They also offer advice and support for parents, often providing classes in parenting skills.

Private

Private services are provided by businesses that make a profit. Private provision includes private day nurseries or private schools. Some day nurseries will take children aged 6 months or even younger. Parents have to pay for this type of care.

Childminders who look after children in their own home come under this heading, and again parents have to pay.

Nannies look after children in the children's own home for pay. Sometimes the nanny lives in the child's home.

Crèches are where parents can leave their children, for example while they study or go to work. Sometimes the parents get help towards payment.

A nanny is paid to look after children in their own home

Playgroups can be a good way to get children used to each other's company before they start school

Voluntary

This sector is funded by charities, and parents have to pay to have their children cared for.

Pre-school playgroups

These provide sessions usually either in a morning or an afternoon for children between 2½ and 5 years old.

The sessions are usually held in community centres or church halls and are managed by parents who have completed training. There is usually a charge to help pay staff wages and help provide craft materials and toys.

Parent and toddler groups

In parent and toddler groups, parents and children remain together.

These groups give children a chance to mix with other children and parents to have the company of other parents. There is usually a small charge to cover rent and a cup of tea.

In a parent and toddler group, a child can play with other children and stay close to a familiar adult

Choosing play provision

Because there are so many types of play provision to choose from, you need to find out as much as you can about them.

There are many things you may be worried about as a parent:

- Cost – does all the money have to be paid at once?
- Do I pay for the session even if the child doesn't go?
- Are the staff trained?
- Does my child need anything with them?
- Can my child take their dummy in with them?
- Can I stay with my child?
- When do I leave my child?
- What will my child do there?

It may be the first time the child has been away from their main carer. It can be scary meeting all those new children and adults. You will need to give lots of support to the child.

Adults can make new friends at playgroup too!

Benefits of play provision for the child:

- meeting other children and making new friends
- new toys to play with
- learning to share
- doing different things like painting, gluing and sticking
- learning new songs
- listening to stories
- learning to follow someone else's rules
- having fun
- learning to play board games
- going on trips
- sports day.

Benefits to parents:

- time to do jobs at home like tidying up or ironing
- a chance to share problems with other parents
- making new friends
- a little bit of peace and quiet
- time to get college work done if on a course
- time for a coffee with friends
- doing shopping.

Some parents stay and help, and sometimes they enjoy it so much that they go to college and do a childcare course, so they can get a job looking after children.

Summary of Unit 3

- Play is important for babies and young children, as it is through play that they learn all about the world around them.
- Children need to experience lots of different activities – playing with different materials like sand and water, toys suitable for their age and stage of development.
- Children and babies need adults to make sure they are kept safe when playing and that the toys they are given are safe.
- Adults need to be good role models, as children will copy what adults do and say.
- Children need lots of praise for good behaviour so they will act the same way again.
- Adults need to praise children so that children feel valued.
- TV programmes and DVDs need to be checked to make sure they are suitable for children.
- It is important that adults listen to what children are saying.